DOGS SET V

Irish Setters

Julie Murray
ABDO Publishing Company

visit us at
www.abdopub.com

Published by ABDO Publishing Company, 4940 Viking Drive, Edina, Minnesota 55435.
Copyright © 2003 by Abdo Consulting Group, Inc. International copyrights reserved in
all countries. No part of this book may be reproduced in any form without written
permission from the publisher.

Printed in the United States.

Cover Photo: Animals Animals
Interior Photos: Animals Animals pp. 7, 11, 13, 21; Corbis pp. 5, 9, 15, 17, 19

Contributing Editors: Kate A. Conley, Kristin Van Cleaf, Kristianne E. Vieregger
Art Direction & Graphics: Neil Klinepier

Library of Congress Cataloging-in-Publication Data

Murray, Julie, 1969-
     Irish setters / Julie Murray.
         p. cm. -- (Dogs. Set V)
     Summary: An introduction to the physical characteristics, behavior, and proper care
of Irish Setters.
     Includes bibliographical references (p.).
     ISBN 1-57765-924-4
     1. Irish setters--Juvenile literature. [1. Irish setters. 2. Dogs.] I. Title.

SF429.I7 M87 2003
636.752'6--dc21

                                                                    2002074658

Contents

The Dog Family

Dogs and humans have been living together for thousands of years. Dogs were first tamed about 12,000 years ago. They were used as guards, hunters, and companions.

Today, about 400 different dog **breeds** exist. They can differ greatly in appearance. Some can weigh as much as 200 pounds (91 kg). Others are small enough to fit in the palms of your hands.

Despite these differences, all dogs belong to the same scientific **family**. It is called Canidae. The name comes from the Latin word *canis*, which means dog.

The Canidae family includes more than just **domestic** dogs. Foxes, jackals, coyotes, and wolves belong to the Canidae family, too. In fact, many people believe today's domestic dogs descended from wolves.

This red fox and other members of the Canidae family are related to the Irish setter.

Irish Setters

Irish setters were first **bred** in Ireland in the 1800s. They are probably a combination of several breeds. These breeds may include English setters, Gordon setters, and pointers.

Originally, Irish setters were bred to hunt. They found **game** birds for hunters without scaring the birds into flight. This was called "setting the game." It is how Irish setters received their name.

The Irish setter breed came to the United States in 1875. Irish setters soon became popular pets known for their beauty. President Harry Truman owned an Irish setter called Mike. President Richard Nixon had an Irish setter named King Timahoe.

Irish setters were once known as the "red spaniel" in Ireland. Today, they are sometimes called the "red setter" or "big red."

What They're Like

Irish setters are good pets and excellent hunting dogs. They are highly active and need regular exercise. Lack of exercise will lead Irish setters into mischief.

Irish setters develop more slowly than other dog **breeds**. They do not fully develop until they are two to three years old. This makes Irish setters appear clumsy and uncoordinated when young.

Young Irish setters need strict training and patience. If they are allowed to behave as they wish, Irish setters will get into trouble. But as they grow, they become strong, intelligent, and fun-loving dogs.

The Irish setter is an outgoing, happy dog.

Coat and Color

The Irish setter's coat is medium length. It lies flat on the dog's body. A healthy coat is silky and shiny.

The Irish setter has short, fine hair on its head. The stomach, ears, and back of the legs all have long, silky, feathering hair. The hair on its tail is long. This hair **tapers** all the way to the tail's tip.

An Irish setter's coat can range in color from chestnut red to deep **mahogany**. Sometimes, an Irish setter may have white patches on its throat, chest, head, or toes.

Opposite page: The Irish setter's shiny coat and deep red color attract many people to the breed.

Size

The Irish setter is a large **breed**. A male stands about 27 inches (69 cm) tall at the shoulders. It weighs about 70 pounds (32 kg). A female measures about 25 inches (64 cm) at the shoulders. It weighs about 60 pounds (27 kg).

In addition to being large, the Irish setter is also long and sleek. Its body is longer than it is tall! An Irish setter has long, muscular legs with small paws. Its neck is long, strong, and slightly **arched**.

The Irish setter also has long, low-set ears that hang close to its head. It carries its tail straight behind its body. The Irish setter also has dark, almond-shaped eyes and a black or chocolate-colored nose.

Opposite page: A full-grown Irish setter